(previous page)
A young deacon participating in the annual *Timqat*, or Epiphany, celebration, held to commemorate the Baptism of Christ. He is holding a church umbrella.

(opposite)
The annual celebration of Giyorgis, or St George's Day, at Bét Giyorgis (St George's church), Lalibela, in the north of the country. Bét is Amharic for 'house'. Festivities for St George are held on the 23rd of every Ethiopian month, but the most important celebration takes place every year at the annual feast, in April.

One afternoon in the Danakil desert, in the north-east of the country, women remained in their hut during a sandstorm brought on by the hot wind. This is a country of salt plains and lava, where the land falls below sea level. The desert here is one of the hottest and most forbidding in the world.

The dance of the Hamar people, who live in the savanna of the Omo River basin in south-west Ethiopia. A remote land, far from the centre of government, it is a region where age-old African customs are still practised. Note painted faces, leather clothing, metal necklaces, bracelets, armlets, leg decorations and cowry-shell decorations.

BLESS ETHIOPIA

Photography by Kazuyoshi Nomachi

Introduction by Richard Pankhurst

© 1998 Odyssey Publications Limited and
PPS (Pacific Press Service Limited, Tokyo)

Photography and captions © 1998 Kazuyoshi Nomachi represented by
PPS (Pacific Press Service Limited, Tokyo)

Text © 1998 Odyssey Publications Limited

Distributed in the United States of America by W.W. Norton & Company, Inc.,
New York

Library of Congress Catalog Card Number has been requested.

Odyssey Publications Limited
1004 Kowloon Centre, Ashley Road, Kowloon, Hong Kong
Tel: (852) 2856 3896   Fax: (852) 2565 8004
E-mail: odyssey@asiaonline.net

Editors: Julie Gaw and Martha Dahlen
Editorial Co-ordinator: Margaret Lam
Design: Yuki Nakajo and Bruno Lee
Jacket Design: Margaret Lee
Maps: Shoichiro Masuda

Translation of the captions from Japanese by Kumi Masunaga

Editors' note: Many systems of transliteration exist for Ethiopian words,
names and places. Where possible, we have opted for 'common' or 'popular'
spellings and have tried to use these consistently rather than attempting
to give definitive spellings, which would be beyond the scope of this work.

ISBN 962-217-518-X

Printed and bound in Hong Kong

98 99 00 01 02   5 4 3 2 1

PREFACE

BY KAZUYOSHI NOMACHI

It is early morning. A group of pilgrims quietly descend a stairway of stone to an underground church to pray. Both men and women wear tattered cotton clothes; they are barefoot. At the bottom of the steps, from out of the dark, tired hands stretch up as a voice begs, 'Sella Mariam, Sella Krestos...' (Mary, Christ, please show us mercy...)

In the church, beeswax candles burn palely along the walls, giving faint light. Sacred songs with a unique melody and slow tempo are being sung, accompanied by the heavy sound of drums. A girl prays, in spiritual rapture, as she kisses the smooth entrance wall, polished by the hands of thousands. The fragrance of incense wafts from the far side... the sights, the sounds, the smells, all evoke a mysterious atmosphere reminiscent of a festival day in Jerusalem 2,000 years ago.

The first time I visited Lalibela—sacred land perched on a mountain 2,600 metres above sea level in the north-east of Ethiopia—was January 1981. Their world of prayers seemed so far removed from the modern time of the end of the 20th century that Lalibela seemed to have dropped out of the great wheel of history. Compared to other places I had seen in Africa, it was unique.

Geographically, Ethiopia sits astride a rift in the crust of the earth's surface. The crustal activity here—which continues to tear the African continent—not only created the Great Rift Valley dividing Ethiopia in half but also created a diverse geography, with man's habitat ranging from highland of 3,500 metres above sea level to searing desert of 100 metres below sea level.

In this rough land, many groups of people live, speaking 80 languages, practising various religions, and maintaining a huge diversity of cultures intact. Where gorges divide the landscape, it is common to find groups with different languages living only a gorge away from each other. Among these are the Falashas, the Black Jews, whose ancestors came from Israel 3,000 years ago and, according to legend, brought with them God's Ark.

The lowlands are a sea of Islam, while the highlands are an island of Christianity. At the same time, in the south-west savanna, certain stock farmers of Nile ancestry maintain their own religion. And there are groups in the River Omo basin who live as 'the last people of Africa' without the need of clothing.

But diversity has its costs. Ethiopia, so diverse it could be called a microcosm of the entire African continent, has had to face many trials due to the complexity of the divisions of its people. In the past 30 years, revolution, civil war, drought, and famine have all taken their toll.

So, what captivated me and drew me back to Ethiopia, again and again?

Was it to see the living accumulation of 3,000 years of history... the lights and shadows of a unique culture preserved by its geographical isolation and maintained through generations by its compelling force... reverence for God stemming from deep spiritual faith... heartfelt emotions richly evident as people together eke out a frugal existence...?

Perhaps it was to see, again and again, how these people bear the sorrow which every human bears. For Ethiopia's sorrow is like the clear and dry sky of the African highland; no clouds of gloom or poverty spoil the clarity of the vision.

A foreign land, Ethiopia, a land of humans with life-sized shadows.

CONTENTS

ERITREA

YEMEN

SUDAN

□ ASMARA

Takkazé

Debra Damo   Korkor Mariam
Adwa   ✚ ● Adigrat   *Dallol*
Aksum   Petros and Pawlos
      Hawzen ✚✚✚   Debra Seyon
Abuna Yemata ✚✚   Debra Salam
              ✚   Wukro
                    ● Mekele
Mt Ras Dashen ▲ 4620   Abba Yohannes
      Semien
      National Park   TEGRAY   *Danakil*
Debra Berhan Selassé   *Desert*   Aseb ●
✚ ● Gondar   Bilbila Giyorgis   DJIBOUTI
Mariam Gemb ✚   ✚ Na'akuto La'ab ● Waldeya
      ● Gorgora   Lalibela ✚
Lake Tana   ✚✚ Gannata Mariam
Ura Kidana Mehrat ✚   ✚ Debra Abuna Aron   Asayta ●   □ DJIBOUTI
Zégé ✚ ▲   *Lake*
Bahr Dar ▲ *Tis Isat Falls*   *Assal*
              Desé ● ● Bati ▲ Hadar   *Lake Abbé*
                    WALLO   *Awash*
GOJJAM   SOMALIA
      ● Bechena
Abbay (Blue Nile) ● Debra Markos   ● Dire Dawa
                                    ● Harar
      ● Debre Berhan

SHEWA

□ ADDIS ABABA   ETHIOPIA

                                       LEGEND
                                       ✚ church

● Arba Minch

Omo ● Jinka

● Konso

● Turmi   ● Yabelo

● Chaw Bét

Lake Turkana

KENYA

The bleak Semien mountains showcase Ethiopia's highest peak, Ras Dashen, at 4,620 metres (15,157 feet) above sea level. The fertile plateau shown here, which is largely cultivated, stands about 3,000 metres (9,842 feet) above sea level. Most of the population are adherents of the Ethiopian Orthodox Church, but there were also some villages of Falashas, or Béta Esra'él, an indigenous group of Judaic Ethiopians, who migrated to Israel, many of them in the 1980s and early 1990s.

INTRODUCTION

BY RICHARD PANKHURST

CHANGING IMAGES OF ETHIOPIA FROM THE OUTSIDE WORLD

Ethiopia, the subject of Kazuyoshi Nomachi's photographic masterpiece, is situated in lofty, historically inaccessible mountains, many located between the Blue Nile and the Red Sea. The country, today a multi-ethnic state, was the site of an ancient, and largely Christian kingdom, whose mysteries have attracted immense fascination from the outside world.

To the ancient Egyptians, the region presented two separate but important images. The first was of the interior, the source of the great River Nile, to whose water and silt the Egyptians owed their existence. The other image was of the Red Sea and Gulf of Aden coast of Africa, which they termed the Land of Punt—God's Land—whence the Pharaohs obtained incense for their religious rites. This territory was so important that Pharaohs despatched expeditions there for over two millennia. The most important was that of Queen Hatshepsut (1501–1479 BC), recorded in stone inscriptions in her temple at Thebes.

To the ancient Greeks who gave Ethiopia its name—the Land of Burnt Faces—it seemed a far-off country. In the ninth century BC, Herodotus declared that it lay at the 'ends of the earth'. In the fifth century, Homer called the place the abode of 'blameless Ethiopians', in communion with their gods. In the fourth century BC, the Ptolemies despatched expeditions along the Red Sea coast in search of elephants, for service in war, thereby reviving Graeco-Egyptian interest in the region.

The minting of coins by the ancient Aksumites during the third century AD, in what is now northern Ethiopia, and the coming of Christianity a century later, introduced the country to the Eastern Roman Empire. This led to correspondence with the Roman Emperor Constantius. The Aksumite conquest, in the early sixth century under King Kaléb, of part of South Arabia further augmented the country's prestige as the most important power between the Eastern Roman Empire and Persia.

To the Arabs in the seventh century, Ethiopia, or Habash, as they named it, was a benevolent country, as to the ancient Greeks. The Prophet Muhammad called it a 'land of righteousness', where 'no one was wronged'. He was not unfamiliar with the country, for his grandfather Abdal Muttalib, who had brought him up, had travelled there on business, while his nanny Baraka was an Ethiopian.

When the Prophet's first disciples were persecuted in Arabia, Muhammad urged them to flee to Habash. Arab envoys came with costly presents to ask the Aksumite ruler to return them. He refused, declaring, 'Even if you were to offer me a mountain of gold, I would not return these people'. Those thus protected included Muhammad's daughter Rokeya, and two women, Umm Habibah and Umm Salma, whom he later married. Muhammad subsequently prayed for the monarch's soul, and exempted the country from the Jihad, or Holy War.

To those in Europe and elsewhere, Ethiopia—also called Abyssinia—was an illustrious realm mentioned in the Bible. Moses had an Ethiopian wife, and her country was mentioned in Psalms 68:31, which prophesied: 'Ethiopia shall soon stretch forth her hands to God'. There were, however, other apparent Biblical allusions. The country was probably the Land of Ophir, whither King Hiram of Tyre had sent for gold, which King Solomon used in building his Temple. Ethiopia was moreover apparently the home of the Queen of the South, known in Ethiopia as Makeda, or Queen of

LALIBELA PILGRIMAGE

Lalibela, situated in the high mountains of Lasta, was founded as a place of Christian pilgrimage in the late 12th or early 13th century by the Ethiopian monarch after whom it was named. For well over half a millennium Ethiopian Christians had gone to worship in Jerusalem, but this entailed a long and arduous journey outside Ethiopia, through desert lands, and involving great risks, from extortionate tax-collectors, slave-traders, thieves and bandits. Many of the faithful therefore doubtless welcomed the founding of Lalibela, which was located well within the Ethiopian Christian realm. Moreover, Lalibela was the site of finely proportioned churches so remarkable in design that not a few traditionally minded people to this day believe that such places of worship could have been made only with the help, or at least approval, of God.

It is therefore perhaps not surprising that Lalibela has long been one of Ethiopia's most important centres of pilgrimage. In the olden days it was visited by numerous men, women, and children who walked, or rode by mule, for days, weeks, or even months on end, and camped around the famous churches. Not a few of today's pilgrims, by contrast, travel by Ethiopian Airlines or four-wheel drive vehicles and stay in modern hotels.

Pilgrims from all over the country journey to Lalibela, as well as to other holy sites, to pray at Christmas, and on other occasions. Many of the faithful, particularly when sick, go to Lalibela to taste, or immerse themselves in, its holy water, and will take bottles of it home to give to their friends and relatives who remain behind. Other devout persons will make vows at Lalibela and other religious sites and, if their wishes are fulfilled, return to give thanks to the Almighty or to their favourite saint.

Ethiopian pilgrimages, to Lalibela and other places of devotion, are profoundly religious events, but also joyous occasions. They break the monotony of traditional country life—and show Ethiopians and foreigners the beauty of what has been called the Ethiopian Wonderland.

(previous pages)
A charismatic monk preaches to pilgrims
gathered for Ethiopian Christmas at
Lalibela. This falls each year on 7th
January. Note the religious painting on
the gnarled old tree, left, the typical
monk's iron staff, surmounted with a
cross, and the crowd of pilgrims dressed
in traditional white cotton clothing
made from a material called *gabbi*.

(opposite)
A group of pilgrims in their cotton
dress—in a few cases somewhat sullied
by their long journey—pass through the
village of Lalibela. Many have trekked
through the mountains for as much as a
fortnight, camping in the open air. They
therefore arrive at the holy site weary, but
full of religious fervour and expectation.

Bét Giyorgis, or St George, is a mono-
lithic rock church cut out of Lalibela's
red volcanic tuff. This historic place of
worship, now largely covered with
lichen, was excavated in the form of a
cross. One of the town's 12 churches,
built by King Lalibela in the late 12th
century, it is 13 metres (43 feet) in
height.

Another view of Bét Giyorgis church.
Note the doors, which are surrounded
by 'monkey heads'. These are representations of the ends of wooden beams,
which would have characterised earlier
structures built of stone and wood.

Bét Giyorgis and part of its surrounding courtyard. Two *tabots*, or symbolic representations of the Biblical Ark of the Covenant, covered in silk and surmounted by brightly coloured umbrellas, are being carried up the church steps. Note elaborate plinth, below the church, and greenish tank of holy water used for ritual immersions.

(above)
Close-up of the two *tabots,* and accompanying umbrellas. Every Ethiopian Christian church possesses one or more *tabots,* or altar slabs. Designed to recall the Biblical Ark, *tabots* are consecrated by the Church, and it is their presence in fact which makes a place of worship holy.

(opposite)
A deacon, with ecclesiastical crown, surmounted by a cross. He is dressed in fine, colourful apparel to accompany the *tabot* on a religious procession. Deacons are often sent by their parents to serve the church, and some later become priests, thus perpetuating the country's age-old Orthodox Christian faith.

(above)

Priests with their crosses and members of the village congregation return to where they will spend the night after placing *tabots* in tents by a pond in an open field. This is a major feature of the traditional *Timqat* celebration. Some ecclesiastics and villagers will remain guarding the tents, with their holy contents, throughout the night.

(opposite)

Bét Mariam, one of the most important of Lalibela's 12 churches, with the morning silhouette of a priest. The excavated land around this church, accessed by several passages and tunnels, forms a sizeable courtyard, where priests, pilgrims and others participate in religious ceremonies.

36

(opposite)
One of many holes in the red volcanic
rock surrounding the Lalibela churches.
Monks reside in these crannies, passing
time. Some come to the holy city to beg
at Christmas and other festivals.

(above)
A deacon reads from the Psalms of David,
or another religious text. This one is
printed on paper, but traditionally it
would have been written on parchment.
The work is in Ge'ez, an Ethiopian
ecclesiastical language, formerly called
Ethiopic in Europe. It is a Semitic tongue
akin to Hebrew and Arabic. Ge'ez is no
longer spoken, or known to the lay
public, but is, like Latin, the root of
several modern vernacular languages.
Note the window which is in the shape
of the decoration surmounting the
famous stele, or obelisks, of Aksum.

(above)
This woman pilgrim has come to the Christmas celebration at Lalibela, all the way from Ethiopia's modern capital, Addis Ababa. The distance of 640 kilometres (398 miles) takes two full days by car.

(opposite)
Two pilgrims pray by the outer wall of Bét Debra Sina. Note two of the many different windows to be seen in the Lalibela church complex. The upper one is modelled on the decorative device of the top of the great obelisks of Aksum. This, like the 'monkey heads' on many Lalibela churches, is illustrative of an on-going Ethiopian architectural tradition.

Courtyard of the church of Bêt Madhané Alam, literally Saviour of the World—the largest of the Lalibela churches—on the morning of Christmas Eve. Prayer started at dawn, but many pilgrims had slept there all night.

(opposite)
Christmas pilgrims camp in the vicinity
of the Madhané Alam church. Simple
farmers, many of them have camped here
for as long as a week, on a frugal diet of
only beans and cereals. Branches and
twigs cut from the nearby mountainside
serve as their beds.

(above)
Pilgrims at dawn in the high land above
Madhané Alam, where prayer is about
to begin.

A group of pilgrims from the Gondar
area pass through a tunnel to Bét Abba
Libanos Church, Lalibela. The journey
from their village, entirely on foot, has
taken them a week.

(opposite)
Young boy standing in front of medieval paintings on a pillar in Bét Marqoréwos church, Lalibela. The figure, top centre, according to local tradition, is King Lalibela. His companions are two other kings of the Zagwé dynasty, Yemrahanna Krestos and Na'akuto La'ab.

(left)
The Star of David, with the Cross of Christ in its centre, on the arched ceiling of Bét Mariam. The combination of the Star and the Cross symbolises the Judaic character of Ethiopian Orthodox Christianity.

(right)
The Virgin Mary, informed of the Immaculate Conception by the Archangel Gabriel, as portrayed in a partly damaged fresco on the corridor of Bét Mariam, Lalibela. Lalibela, one of the wonders of the world, has been recognised as a UNESCO World Heritage site, with restoration now in progress.

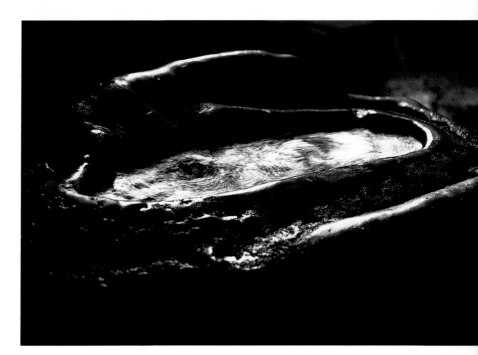

(above)
A pool of Holy Water at the church of Na'akuto La'ab, a church built in a huge cave in the cliff face half an hour's drive east of Lalibela. The water drops constantly from the ceiling, and is taken home to be drunk by the faithful from near and far.

(opposite)
Pilgrims at Bét Mariam. It is a custom of the Ethiopian Orthodox Church that people remove their shoes when entering a church.

(above)
A woman immerses herself in a greenish tank of Holy Water in the courtyard of Bét Mariam. In a state of religious frenzy, she has been lowered by a rope held by one of the priests. Many of the pilgrims watch.

(opposite)
A crowd at Lalibela listens to a priest's sermon. The colourful inverted umbrella, held by a deacon scarcely seen in the picture, is for collecting monetary donations to the church.

The Christmas Service at Lalibela.
Beginning in the late afternoon of
Christmas Eve, when this picture was
taken, the service continues until early
the following morning. Note the turbaned
priests, the costly imported carpets and
church drums, left foreground.

Early next morning, and over 12 hours later. The priests, who have been praying all night, take a well-earned rest. Nearly half of the pilgrims began leaving during the hours of darkness.

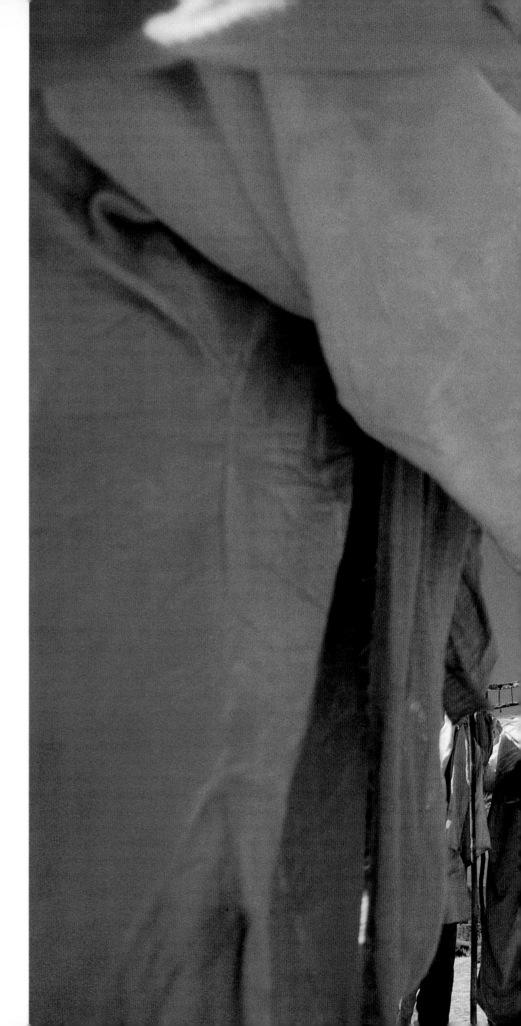

(previous pages)
The church of Bét Mariam on Christmas
morning. Note the priests with their
red-bordered *shammas*, or togas, to the
rear, and to the left, priests with colourful
dress and umbrellas, and two large
paintings of Saints.

(opposite)
Priests, with turbans and colourful robes,
dance in slow ritual in front of the *tabot*
at the *Timqat* celebration. This recalls
the Biblical account in the Second Book
of Samuel 6:5, 14–16, where King David
and the people of Israel dance round the
Ark of the Covenant. Note the priests'
prayer sticks and *sistra*, or church rattles,
which date back to the days of Pharaonic
Egypt. Both are used in conjunction with
Ethiopian Christian chant.

(opposite)
An underground passage connecting the churches of Bét Amanu'él and Bét Abba Libanos. There are scores of such passages and tunnels in the Lalibela church complex.

(above)
Pilgrims assemble beside the main entrance to Bét Gabre'él-Rufa'él church. They have walked over a bridge with a wooden balustrade, to the left of the picture, across a 20-metre (66-foot) precipice.

Pilgrims camping above the church of Bét Madhané Alam. After participating in the Christmas festivities many must trek for as much as a fortnight to reach home.

The Lalibela Cross from Bét Golgotha church, where King Lalibela is believed to have been buried. This distinctive cross is said to have belonged to King Lalibela personally. The upper portion of this cross embodies twelve finials, studded with gold-embossed circles, each said to symbolise one of the Twelve Apostles.

(right)
A devout young woman kissing the cross, which at this point of the elaborate ritual is about to touch her forehead. Priests are almost invariably seen carrying or holding a cross, with which they will bless virtually any member of the community they meet.

(left)
A cross cut out of the rock bed of the Jordan River, at Lalibela. This river, which fills with water only during the rainy season, is called after that in the Bible, and reflects the fact that King Lalibela conceived his capital as a New Jerusalem.

(right)
A woman tattooed with the Cross on her forehead, wearing a silver necklace with amulets. Such tattooing is not uncommon throughout northern Ethiopia.

A monk walks between two gnarled old trees in the vicinity of the Lalibela churches, towards a cave popularly known as the Grave of Adam. The rock churches themselves are located in excavated land to the rear of the picture.

67

Two pilgrims at their Lalibela camp at sunset. The atmosphere, little touched by the modern world, is still reminiscent of medieval times, when the churches were originally conceived.

LIFE IN THE HIGHLANDS

Ethiopia, a mountainous country, has land at many different altitudes, and hence varying temperatures and climates. The highlands, the abode of most of the population, contain some of the most beautiful sights in the entire country.

Much of the highland area is also particularly fertile. This was noticed by the early 16th century Portuguese traveller Francisco Alvares. Passing through the highlands of southern Tegray, he reports that the people there told him that there was 'so much cultivation of all kinds' that each year they had gathered so much corn of all kinds that, were it not for the weevil, 'there would have been abundance for ten years. And because I was amazed they said to me, "Honoured guest, do not be amazed, because in the years that we harvest little we gather enough for three years' plenty in the country; and were it not for the multitude of locusts and the hail which sometimes do great damage, we should not sow the half of what we sow, because the yield is incredibly great; so it is sowing wheat, barley, lentils, pulse or any other seed. And we sow so much with the hope that even if any of those said plagues should come, some would be spoiled, and some would remain, and, if all is spoiled, the year before has been so plentiful that we have no scarcity"'.

A similar picture was drawn at the turn of the 17th century by the French physician Charles Poncet. 'There is no country,' he exclaimed, 'better peopled or more fertile than Aethiopia. All the fields, and even the mountains (of which there are a great number) are well cultivated'.

Livestock, traditionally, was likewise plentiful. Towards the end of the 18th century the Scottish traveller James Bruce thus reported that he saw 'plenty' of cows and bulls 'of exquisite beauty'.

Morning in a village near the Semien
mountains. In villages like this, rarely
visited by cars, the day starts only with
the noise and bustle of people and cattle.

Reed boats, locally known as *tankwas*, used on Lake Tana, in the north-west of the country. Such boats, made from papyrus stems growing by the lake shore, date back to the time of the Pharaohs in Egypt. Those in this picture, however, are of a more recent and exceptionally wide design, used for the bulk transportation of fuel-wood to the lakeside town of Bahr Dar.

A *tankwas*, of a more traditional design, on Lake Tana. It belongs to a local lake-side people, known as the Wayto, who propel their craft with the help of paddles. *Tankwas* do not last long. The papyrus, from which they are made, soon becomes water-logged. The boats are put in the sun to dry, but must be replaced before long.

The present-day village of Lalibela, stretching out across the flat mountain slopes above the famous 800-year-old rock churches. The settlement, except for the modern tourist hotels, is today still largely without electricity, but several four-wheeled vehicles can be seen in the picture. Note corrugated iron roofing and eucalyptus trees, both characteristic features of many Ethiopian settlements today.

Barefooted men in a simple village bar
drink *talla*, a refreshing beer made from
local grains.

The proprietress of another rural drinking establishment, with her son. Note simple furniture, and, on the wall, a traditional style Ethiopian painting depicting rural life, as well as two cautionary texts. One states, 'whereas one can taste sugar or salt, one cannot tell in advance whom one can trust'. The other says, 'however bad things become, breakfast can never be considered as lunch'.

Several villagers assemble at a weekly market. Some travel for miles to buy or sell; others to exchange information, or merely to gossip.

(*above*)
A young girl cooking one of the staple foods of Ethiopia, *enjera*, which is made from a grain called *tef*, ground to powder and fermented. *Tef* resembles millet and is grown only in the Ethiopian highlands.

(*opposite*)
Adaré women chewing *chat* leaves, said to alleviate hunger and tiredness and promote abundant vitality. Its regular use is widespread throughout Eastern Africa and Yemen. In Harar, a famous centre for *chat* leaves, people spend the afternoon burning incense and smoking water pipes.

The great waterfall of the Blue Nile, known in Ethiopia as the Abbay, in the north-west of the country. These falls are called in Amharic the Chis-Abbay, literally 'Smoke-Abbay'. After the falls, the river flows almost entirely around the Ethiopian region of Gojjam before joining the White Nile at Khartoum, in Sudan, and then proceeds on its way to Egypt.

CHURCHES IN ROCK

Ethiopia, one of the first lands to adopt Christianity, is an immense country with over 30,000 churches, and more than 1,000 monasteries. Small parish churches are found throughout the Christian highlands, but others are situated in more remote areas, notably on the islands of Lake Tana, and in the rugged mountains of the north.

The tradition of rock excavation in Ethiopia dates back to ancient times, when a significant part of the population lived in caves. Later, after the coming of Christianity, it became customary to cut churches out of the living rock. Such churches exist all over the country: from the vicinity of Keren, in Eritrea in the north, to the neighbourhood of Goba, in Balé in the far south. Though the greatest concentration of rock churches are in Lalibela, the largest number are in Tegray and two can also be seen in the Addis Ababa area. There can be no doubt that many other such places of worship await discovery in the years ahead. Some of the earliest rock churches date back to the earliest years of Christianity, while three were, remarkably enough, dug out only in the last decade or so.

Three different types of rock church can be discerned. One type features structures which have been dug out from the rock on all sides, leaving the place of worship fully separated from the surrounding land on all sides by a narrow trench or space. A second type features churches dug out only in the front, or on one or more sides, with the back still entirely attached to the original rock. The interiors of both of both these kinds of church are also hewn from within, to resemble an ordinary church. A third type features edifices built of stone and wood rather than dug out, but situated within large caves which afford them protection from hostile attack as well as inclement weather.

(left)
Abuna Yemata church, at Guh, in the Tegray district of Garalta. One of the most inaccessible places of worship in the entire region, it can be reached only after a precipitous one-hour climb. This takes one past a cave, centre, in which there are a number of skeletons, while using the dead trees as a hand rail. The entrance to the church is to the left of the pillar, behind the man further left. The church is named after Abuna Yemata, one of the Nine Saints—holy Greek-speaking men from Syria, who came to Ethiopia in the late fifth or early sixth centuries, and were instrumental in establishing a number of monasteries in the north of the country. The word *Abun*, literally Our Father, is an honorific term applied to a high ecclesiastic.

(right)
The highly decorated interior of Abuna Yemata church, with very unusual 15th or 16th century paintings. Those on the south dome are eight of the Twelve Apostles, plus the Lord's brother James. Anti-clockwise, from the figure with the white robes and brown turban, the inscriptions identify them as Matthias, James, John, James the brother of Christ, Thaddeus, Andrew, Philip, Bartholomew and Nathaniel. Paul, Peter and Thomas are depicted on the far right, below the dome.

(left)
Enoch, known in Ethiopia as Hénok, left, and Elijah, right, with Musé, or Moses, just off the picture, far right.

(right)
Eight of the so-called Nine Saints, depicted in the northern dome. The ninth, Abuna Yemata himself to whom the church is dedicated, is seen elsewhere. Only seven of the eight are in fact named. They are, beginning anti-clockwise from the man, top right, without a turban: Abba Liqanos, Abba Garima, Abba Pantaléwon, Abba Sehma, Abba Guba, Abba Aragawi and Abba Afsé.

Another view of the church of Abuna Yemata. The saint is depicted, on horseback, immediately above the two standing priests.

(top)
Debra Damo, one of Ethiopia's oldest and most renowned monasteries, was founded in the sixth century by Abba Aragawi, one of the Nine Saints. The monastery stands on an isolated and largely inaccessible *amba*, or mountain plateau, in northern Tegray. The monks are in their ceremonial robes to celebrate the beginning of the great Easter fast, which in Ethiopia lasts no less than 56 days. Note the building's use of stones, without any mortar or cement, and the presence of 'monkey heads' akin to those reproduced in stone on the Lalibela churches.

(bottom)
Debra Damo can be reached only by a hair-raising 15-metre (49-foot) perpendicular climb. This is assisted, as in the picture, by a rope pulled from the summit by friendly monks.

Bells made from basalt stone are struck by a monk at Abba Yohannes. Their tone depends on their size and shape. Such bells can be seen at many an old-time Ethiopian church.

(above)
A wall painting of an elephant on the church of Mika'él, or St Michael, at Debra Salam, in the Tegray district of Atsbi. Elephants were known throughout Ethiopian history, but the personality depicted is probably St Thomas of India, whose life was well known to Ethiopian medieval scholars.

(opposite)
A Debra Damo priest reads from the New Testament. Printed texts such as this are gradually replacing traditional manuscripts on parchment. Note priest's colourful robes, and silver processional cross, left.

The church of Gannata Mariam, literally Garden of Mary, on a hill 20 kilometres south-east of Lalibela. This church, the roof of which is decorated with crosses, dates from the 13th century. It is 20 metres (66 feet) long, 16 metres (52 feet) wide and 11 metres (36 feet) high, and has a long and wide corridor within the massive pillars. In the front right of the main picture, a group of nuns clean grain prior to cooking it.

The rock-hewn church of Abuna Aron, in the monastery of that name at Maqét, 60 kilometres (37 miles) south-west of Lalibela. A streak of light enters every day through a vertical hole in the roof, for about a quarter of an hour, just after midday, but it is said that not a drop of rain comes in, even during the heaviest downpours of the rainy season. Three monks can be seen reading by this light from a parchment manuscript. The picture above depicts monks holding candles in the gloom before the almost miraculous entry of the light.

(opposite)

The interior of Mariam church at Korkor. This place of worship, which is 16 metres (52 feet) long, 16 metres (52 feet) wide and six metres (20 feet) high, is reached by climbing for an hour and a half on the side of the precipice opposite that where Abuna Yemata church stands.

(left)

A picture of Eve, with the serpent, beside the Tree of Knowledge, on the wall of Mariam church, Korkor. This is a close-up of the picture high above the priest on the opposite page.

(right)

A medieval painted fan, at Mariam church at Debra Seyon, in the Tegray district of Garalta. This fan, made of over 30 pieces of parchment, depicts the Virgin Mary and the Christ Child, top, the Twelve Apostles, right, and other Biblical personalities.

(left)

A young village girl, tattooed with a cross, stands in the church of Pétros and Pawlos (Peter and Paul), at Malahayenghi, in the district of Wukro, in Tegray. The church, which has largely fallen into ruins, is situated on the top of a steep precipice, difficult to climb. The *tabot* and other church property has therefore been transferred to a newly built rock church.

(right)

The famous ceiling, depicting winged angels, at the church of Debra Berhan Sellasé at Gondar. This church, the walls of which are also covered with paintings, was founded by Emperor Iyasu I in the late 17th century, but was rebuilt in the early 19th century. The eyes of the angels have been so painted as to appear to be staring at everyone in the church below.

Blind priests are often to be seen in
Ethiopia. The service of God is virtually
the only occupation open to the physically
handicapped, for whom the only other
available occupation, employment in
agriculture, would be impossible. Many
priests, after the death of their spouse,
opt to become monks. Note typical
monk's cap, and iron cross, above.

Bilbila Giyorgis, or St George's Church, in the district of Bilbila, 30 kilometres (19 miles) north-west of Lalibela. This church is excavated only in the front, and is often surrounded by a swarm of supposedly sacred bees. Like many other old places of worship, it is in urgent need of restoration. It is hoped that in view of Ethiopia's rich cultural heritage and current lack of resources, the help of the international community can be mobilised for such restoration work.

Powder made from crushed rocks near
Bilbila Giyorgis is believed to be a valuable
skin treatment. Women may sometimes
be seen entirely naked attempting this cure.

Priest standing in Mariam Gemb church, at the entrance to the *Maqdes*, or Holy of Holies. Only ordained priests are allowed to enter this portion of the church, where the *tabot*, or symbolic representation of the Ark of the Covenant, is kept. The church is covered with paintings, and once again, 'monkey heads', or representation of beam ends, round the doors. Also displayed are cheap religious prints imported from abroad. Efforts are currently being made to remove such prints, which add nothing to a church's distinction.

The famous obelisks of Aksum are believed to date from the early fourth century, immediately prior to the advent of Christianity around 300 AD. One of these remarkable structures was looted on the personal orders of the Italian Fascist dictator Benito Mussolini, and taken to Rome in 1937. The broken obelisk, in the front of the picture, was the largest single piece of stone ever worked by humanity. The local authorities in Tegray, the region where it is situated, have requested its re-erection.

Many of the Aksum obelisks, excavated from a mountain five kilometres (three miles) outside the city, collapsed over the centuries, and shattered in falling. Here a young girl has come with a plastic Jerry can to collect water beside one of the obelisks.

(above)
A *tabot*, or symbolic representation of
the Ark of the Covenant, taken out of
its church for the *Timqat*, or Epiphany,
festival, which recalls the Baptism of
Christ. On such occasions *tabots* are
invariably covered in costly silks, and

carried on the heads of priests,
protected by colourful umbrellas. They
are then taken to a tent near a river,
lake or other expanse of water, where
they spend the night.

(opposite)
Blessing the water as part of the *Timqat*
celebrations. Three candles have been
lit. No sooner had this been done, and
the officiating priest finished his prayers,
than youngsters and others rushed to
immerse themselves in the holy water.

A procession of *tabots* gathered together for the festivities. Note method of carrying, and the umbrellas.

121

(above)

The *Masqal,* literally Cross, Festival, is held every year in September. Celebrated throughout Christian Ethiopia, this festival commemorates the discovery of the True Cross, on which Christ was crucified, at the time of the Eastern Empress Helena, mother of the eastern Roman Emperor Constantine the Great. On the eve of this celebration a bonfire is lit, around which people sing and dance. This picture shows a group of young girls dancing prior to the lighting of the fire.

(opposite)
The *Masqal* fire ablaze.

Entrance to *Maqdes*, or Holy of Holies, of Ura Kidana Mehrat Church, on the Zégé peninsula by Lake Tana. Situated within easy boat ride of the modern lakeside town of Bahr Dar, the peninsula has been the site, for centuries, of coffee cultivation. Note painting featuring winged angels.

THE 'SOLOMONIC PERIOD'

Opposition to Zagwé rule by the neighbouring provinces of Tegray, Amhara and Shewa crystallised around prominent churchmen related to the Shewan prince Yekuno Amlak. This led to the overthrow of the Zagwés around 1270, and another major shift in the centre of political power, southwards to Shewa. There Yekuno Amlak established a new dynasty, which claimed descent from Solomon and the Queen of Sheba, and dominated Ethiopia for seven centuries.

Yekuno Amlak claimed descent from both Delna'od, the last king of Aksum, and from Menilek I, the son of Solomon and the Queen of Sheba. This claim later found expression in the *Kebra Nagast,* or *Glory of Kings,* which was written in Ge'ez during the reign of Yekuno Amlak's grandson, Amda Seyon (1312–42). The text was based on the First Book of Kings 10:1–13.

The *Kebra Nagast* tells how the Ark of the Covenant is supposed to have reached Ethiopia. The text claims that Makeda, Queen of Sheba, visited Solomon to learn of his wisdom, accepted his religion, and was then prevailed upon, by a stratagem, to share his bed, so that he could 'work his will with her'. He then allegedly dreamt that he saw the sun, which had shone over Israel, move to Ethiopia, over which it shone evermore.

The queen then supposedly returned to Ethiopia, where she gave birth to Menilek, her son by Solomon. The child, on attaining manhood, travelled to Jerusalem to meet his father, who recognised him as his first-born and begged him to stay in Israel. The young man, however, insisted on returning to his mother. Solomon agreed, but gave him the first-born of his leading courtiers and clerics to accompany him. Reluctant to leave without divine protection, they abducted the Ark. Menilek, on being informed, declared that since God had allowed this to happen it must have been His wish that the Ark be taken to Ethiopia.

Another Ethiopian version of the legend claims that the Ethiopians had formerly worshipped a serpent, to whom they annually gave a young girl as tribute. Angabo, a stranger, eventually offered to eliminate the reptile, if the people agreed to make him king. A pact was concluded, after which he poisoned the snake, cut off its head, and was duly crowned. He was subsequently succeeded by his daughter, the Queen of Sheba. This legend is presented in 20th century 'strip cartoons' produced to this day.

The *Kebra Nagast* embodied a powerful message. Makeda's association with Solomon, and the birth of their son Menilek, showed that the rulers of Ethiopia deserved special respect and obedience, as descendants of the Biblical kings of Israel. Solomon's dream, followed by Ethiopia's acquisition of the Ark—supposedly by God's wish—likewise indicated that the Ethiopians had replaced the Jews as God's chosen people.

Such beliefs were adopted by the country's royal chronicles, which began to be written in the early 14th century during the reign of Emperor Amda Seyon. They present the Almighty as the Old Testament God of War, and the king of Ethiopia as His chosen instrument.

The early 'Solomonic' period witnessed an important growth in Ge'ez literature. This included the country's earliest real work of history: an elaborate account of Amda Seyon's victories over Muslim adversaries to the East. This was the first of a series of royal chronicles, which were written until modern times. Almost unparalleled in Africa, they provide an almost unbroken narrative covering virtually seven centuries.

Another important work produced during Amda Seyon's reign was the country's legal code, the *Fetha Nagast,* or *Law of Kings*. Translated into Ge'ez from a Coptic Arabic text, and based largely on Biblical writ, it codified contemporary legal beliefs, including the divine right of kings and the right to own slaves. This code remained in use until the early 20th century.

Not a few other Ge'ez literary works were also produced during the 15th century, notably several by Emperor Zar'a Ya'qob (1433–1468), a life-long devotee of the Virgin Mary. Other works composed in her honour included the *Miracles of Mary*. The period also saw the composition of *Acts*, or *Lives*, of numerous holy men.

Ethiopian Saints are depicted according to strictly stylised iconography. Takla Haymanot is thus shown with wings, standing on one leg. Gabra Manfus is dressed in a costume of feathers, a bird drinking from his eye, and lions and leopards on either side of him. Aragawi is carried to the summit of his monastery at Dabra Damo by a snake. Samuél of Waldebba rides on a lion. St George, riding on a horse, spears a dragon to rescue a damsel. She is called Brutawit, literally the girl from Beirut.

MEDIEVAL LIFE

Ethiopian medieval rulers exercised immense powers, which were established in the *Fetha Nagast,* or *Law of Kings*. These were so considerable that Emperor Zar'a Ya'qob is said by his chronicler to have inspired 'great terror among the people', who, 'trembled' before him.

Rulers were often accompanied by innumerable soldiers and camp-followers, and spent much of their time on tours of inspection, collecting taxes or waging war.

Military service was related to land tenure. Vassals held land in return for service in war. Vast numbers of warriors could be mobilised with remarkable speed. Alvares reported that 100,000 men could be rallied in two days.

Soldiers seized whatever they wanted from the peasantry. The chronicle of Emperor Eskender (1478–94) admits that his soldiers 'ruined all the people'. Depredations were so considerable that the Florentine trader Andrea Corsali observed, in 1517, that Emperor Lebna Dengel's army was so large that it could not remain anywhere for more than four months, or return in less than ten years. Changes in the location of capitals often resulted from the soldiers' destruction of forests.

The monarch's powers covered both land tenure and taxation. Emperors could grant revenue from any piece of land, by waiving their rights in favour of others: members of their family, nobles, local chiefs, the priesthood or religious establishments. Such land was known as *gult*, and gave its owner the tribute otherwise paid to the ruler. Dues were usually provided in kind: cattle, grain, honey, butter or labour services. These included ploughing, harvesting and threshing, building and repairing palaces, and preparation of banquets.

Peasants, however, generally owned their own land, which was known as *rest*, and was inherited. The monarch could grant *gult* rights to such land, but could not expropriate *rest*-owners, except in very special circumstances, in case for example of treason.

The Ethiopian Church and its Coptic Patriarch enjoyed immense wealth and influence. Important churches and monasteries were endowed with extensive lands. The Patriarch also owned considerable property. Though a foreigner, he often played a major role in state affairs.

The economy was largely self-sufficient. Trade largely took the form of barter, or was based on such 'primitive money' as bars of salt, pieces of cloth or strips of iron. Farmers and other land-holders paid their taxes to their local chief in kind, mainly in grain or cattle. Honey and butter also served as articles of tribute. Major provincial taxes, on the other hand, were usually paid in gold, which was locally panned, and obtained from Enarya in the south-west. The metal was weighed on hand scales, often against imported coins, which served as units of weight.

The monarchy, though powerful, suffered from major weaknesses over the succession. Rulers often had several wives, and their children had virtually equal claim to the throne. Conflicts among heirs were therefore not infrequent. Another difficulty was that minors were often selected to reign, because the nobility liked child kings, whom they could manipulate.

To protect the society from disputes over succession, unwanted royal aspirants to the throne were often placed in detention. This practice dated back to Aksumite times, when the mountain of Debra Damo served as a royal prison. It was replaced in the medieval period by Amba Geshen, a flat-topped mountain in Shewa.

THE CRENELLATED PALACES OF GONDAR

A new phase of Ethiopian history opened in 1636, with the establishment, by Emperor Fasiladas (1632–67), of his headquarters at Gondar. The town, which remained the capital for over two centuries, was well situated, for it enjoyed access to the rich lands south of the Blue Nile, as well as to major trade routes, to Sudan and the port of Massawa.

At Gondar, Fasiladas built a palace, known as the Fasil Gemb, or Fasil building. Larger and more impressive than any then erected, it was described around 1648 by a Yamani envoy, Hasan ibn al-Haymi, as among the 'most beautiful of glorious marvels'. Reportedly designed by an Indian, this palace was stoutly built with stone and mortar, in the form of a crenellated castle. Like his predecessors, the monarch spent much time on campaign, but returned to his palace during the rains.

Fasiladas was succeeded in 1667 by his son Yohannes I, and in 1682, by his grandson Iyasu I, both of whom built further palaces. The reigns of the first three Gondarine rulers thus witnessed the emergence of a sizeable imperial quarter, later surrounded by a strong stone wall.

The city also had several dozen churches. One of the finest, founded by Emperor Iyasu I, was Debra Berhan Sellasé. Originally rectangular, it was rebuilt, in the early 19th century, as a round church. It is renowned for its beautiful paintings, and ceiling decorated with winged angels.

Gondar was not only the political capital, but also a major commercial and religious centre. The city's trade was largely in the hands of Muslims, who lived in their own distinct settlement. Known as Eslam Bét (bét being the Amharic for 'house'), it was located in lower land near the confluence of the rivers Qaha and Angerab.

The city's population included numerous priests and other ecclesiastics. The two most important were the Egyptian Coptic Abun, or Patriarch, and the Ethiopian Echagé, or Head of the Monks. Both had extensive establishments which were places of asylum, where criminals were exempt from arrest.

Gondar was also a major handicraft centre. Most artisans belonged to minority groups, either Falasha, or Muslim. The Falashas lived outside the town, beyond the Qaha river. Their menfolk worked mainly as blacksmiths and weavers, and their women as potters. There were also a number of Falasha masons engaged in both palace and church-building. The Muslims, on the other hand, were mainly weavers, tent-makers and tent-carriers for the army.

Gondar witnessed a major renaissance after the accession, in 1721, of Emperor Bakaffa. Empress Mentewab—his wife and later, his widow—erected a beautiful palace to the north of the royal compound. A two-storey crenellated structure, its walls were profusely ornamented with red Ethiopian-style crosses.

Mentewab's son, Emperor Iyasu II, also took a keen interest in palace building. He redecorated the old Fasil Gemb with the help of Greeks from Asia Minor, who had fled their native land, and included 12 silversmiths 'very excellent' at filigree work.

Mentewab also erected several buildings in the hills north-west of Gondar. This area, known as Qwesqwam, was called after the place in Egypt where the Virgin Mary supposedly resided.

Qwesqwam was the site of many royal buildings. The largest, a two-storey palace, was ornamented in red tuff, with crosses, a lioness and elephant, St Samuél of Waldebba riding a lion, and a bearded face said to be that of the then Abun. A smaller nearby building, now ruined, was the private residence of the Empress.

West of the palace, Mentewab erected a remarkably fine circular church, known as Debra Sahay, or Mount of the Sun. According to a chronicle, its roof was surmounted by red cloth which shone like fire, and over 300 mirrors, which flashed like lightning.

In the 18th century, Gondar declined in importance. The empire was disintegrating, and the provinces becoming increasingly independent. Emperors became puppets of feudal leaders, often in conflict with each other. Ethiopian historians called this period the Era of the Judges, because it resembles that in the Book of Judges, 21:25, when 'there was no king in Israel: every man did that which was right in his own eyes'.

THE WALLED CITY OF HARAR

The Muslim walled city of Harar, in the south-east of modern Ethiopia, dates back to early medieval times. Located on an eastern spur of the Ethiopian mountain massif, it enjoyed relatively easy access to the rich lands of the interior, as well as to the ports of Zayla, Tajurah and Berbera.

The city increased in importance, in the early 16th century, under a charismatic leader, Ahmad ibn-Ibrahim, better known as Ahmad Gragn, or the 'left-handed'. He assumed the title of Imam when a swarm of bees, reminiscent of those earlier associated with King Lalibela, settled on his head. Shortly after this he refused to pay tribute to the Ethiopian emperor, and embarked on an attempted conquest of the highlands.

A series of successful expeditions followed, in which he brought back considerable wealth. Gold was so plentiful that it was handed out by the fistful, and a man who gave a gift of 50 ounces had it spurned as a trifle.

The Imam and his followers also captured numerous slaves, which they exported to Arabia. This financed the purchase of firearms, which played a major role in the campaign.

This period also witnessed the reorganisation of Harar's government, administration and taxation. Ahmad claimed that the city's rulers had earlier exploited the populace. He therefore allotted a proportion of the taxes for those in need.

Imam Ahmad was killed in battle in 1543, after which Harar's government was assumed by his nephew, Amir Nur ibn al-Wazir Mujahid, who married his late uncle's widow Bati Del Wambara. It was Nur, according to tradition, who constructed Harar's great encircling wall. His tomb became a place of special veneration.

Harar, thanks to its wall, survived the vicissitudes of time, and remained a major emporium. It was visited by merchants from many lands, while its own traders also travelled far and wide. The rulers of Harar struck their own currency, the only money then produced in this part of Africa. The city also preserved its distinctive culture. This found expression in the Adaré, or Harari, language, a Semitic tongue spoken only within the city. Harar, then and later, was a notable Muslim centre, producing fine Islamic manuscripts which were taken to mosques all over the Horn of Africa.

Despite its commercial, religious and cultural importance, and the many foreign merchants who visited it, Harar was for centuries, to the outside world, a closed and mysterious city. It was not marked on any European map, and virtually nothing was written about it until the early 19th century.

The outside world was indebted for its knowledge of the city to two notable reports. The first was by Ramyat Allah, an Ethiopian trader of eastern Shewa, who lived in Harar for six years in the 1830s, and was interviewed by a British officer, Lieutenant W C Barker. The second account was by the renowned British Orientalist, Richard Burton, who spent ten memorable days at the city in 1855.

Harar, according to these observers, stood on the slope of a hill surrounded by rich, highly cultivated, agricultural land. This stretched, Ramyat declares, 'for miles around', and was in places irrigated with spring water. The surrounding land produced both coffee and the narcotic *chat*, besides wheat, millet, and many fruits and vegetables.

The city, it is evident from the two reports, was larger and more populous than any other settlement on the Horn of Africa. Its houses, according to Ramyat, were 'built very close together', and covered an extensive area that it required two full hours to walk round it quickly.

The old wall, then 200 years old, was, Ramyat states, still well maintained. It averaged three and a half metres (11.5 feet) high and nearly one metre (three feet) thick. Its five gates, Burton reports, were large and 'supported by oval towers', but 'ignorant of cannon'.

The walls, like the buildings within, were made of blocks of granite and sandstone, cemented with clay. The structure, Ranyat says, was 'at all times carefully guarded', and strangers were not allowed to enter without first surrendering their weapons.

Each of the five gates was used by merchants trading with a different area. The Hamaraisa gate, on the west, was used by caravans dealing with the Ethiopian highlands. The Suqutat or Bisidimo gate, to the south-east, by those travelling to and from the fertile province of Arsi. The Bab Bida gate, to the south, handled the Ala Galla caravan; the Argobba gate, to the east, the Berbera caravan; and the Assum or Faldano gate, to the north, the Zayla caravan, which handled the import–export trade.

The city had two main buildings: the great al-Jami mosque, erected by masons from Arabia, and the amir's two-storey palace. According to Burton, the amir's couch, or throne, was decorated with a fine carpet from Persia. The treasury housed 'large hoards of silver, coffee, and ivory', and 'huge boxes of ancient fashion' reportedly full of silver Maria Theresa dollars. The treasurer, chewing *chat*, sat on a large dais, also covered with Persian carpets.

The houses of the common people consisted mainly of long, flat-roofed structures, many two storeys high. The poorest inhabitants lived in thatched huts, like those of the neighbouring peasants.

Most of Harar's male population, according to Ramyat, was occupied in agriculture, and the women in household work. There were, however, many traders whose caravans travelled 'at all seasons'. Those bound for the coast transported coffee, millet, ghee (clarified butter), ostrich feathers and slaves. Imported articles brought to the city included red, white and blue cotton yarns, cheap Indian cloth, mainly blue, European printed cloth, costly silks, shawls, silk thread, beads, zinc and copper wire. The city also handled a considerable quantity of frankincense and other gums from the arid country towards the coast.

Harar was likewise a great centre for handicrafts. It was renowned for its cloth, which, according to Burton, 'in beauty and durability...far surpassed' the 'vapid produce' of European factories. The city's book-binders were also accomplished, so much so that he declared that 'no Eastern country save Persia' surpassed them, in both 'strength and appearance'.

King, later Emperor, Menilek, brought Harar into the then fast modernising Ethiopian state, in 1887. He considered the city so important that he entrusted it to his cousin, Ras Makonnen, who made it the empire's principal eastern outpost and link with the outside world.

Harar was visited at this time by innumerable travellers to the Ethiopian interior. The best known was the French poet Arthur Rimbaud, who had abandoned his literary career to become a merchant. Based in Harar, he dealt in various articles, including firearms, which he supplied to Menilek in the years immediately preceding Menilek's victory at the Battle of Adwa in 1896. A fine house, incorrectly supposed to have been inhabited by the poet-cum-trader, is today a tourist attraction.

The turn of the century witnessed the construction of the Addis Ababa–Djibouti railway. Menilek's original plan was that it should run through Harar. The railway company, however, persuaded him to accept an alternative route through the nearby lowlands. There a new railway town, Dire Dawa, was established.

The coming of the railway had profound consequences for Harar. The old caravan trade based on it declined, as business moved increasingly to Dire Dawa. Harar nevertheless remained a major historical, religious and cultural centre. Devoid of skyscrapers, it retains its old-world charm. Today's visitors, inspecting the city's old houses, narrow winding streets, and stout walls, may well feel they are walking in the footsteps of Ramyat Allah and Arthur Rimbaud.

(continued on page 200)

DANAKIL LOWLANDS

The Danakil, or Afar, lowlands, situated in north-west Ethiopia, are among the most beautiful but inhospitable territories in the world. Traversed with volcanoes, hot springs, and salt lakes, the region is of immense geological interest. Yet, with minimal rainfall, much of the land is uninhabited, with only a stretch of land by the Awash River under cultivation.

The Afar people are largely nomads and almost entirely Muslim by faith. Most are herdsmen tending goats and camels, though some, in more favoured areas, tend cattle. Those with goats and camels migrate long distances in search of scanty herbage; the cattle owners remain for the most part in specific grazing areas. Afars near the coast are, on the other hand, expert fishermen. Many Afars have long been engaged in the mining of rock salt, with which they trade with the highland interior.

Afar huts, which provide shade from the sun, and storage for their owners' meagre possessions, are hemispherical in shape and made of palm ribs covered with matting. Light enough to be transported on camel-back, they are erected in semi-permanent locations in the course of seasonal migrations, usually near wells.

The diet of the Afar people consists chiefly of sour milk and porridge made from *dura* flour. Only at festivals do the Afars eat meat. They also drink an intoxicating potion made from the *dum* palm. Traditionally, Afars lived in isolation, seldom mixing with their neighbours if they could avoid it. Now, however, like other peoples of the country, they increasingly involve themselves in pan-Ethiopian development and other projects.

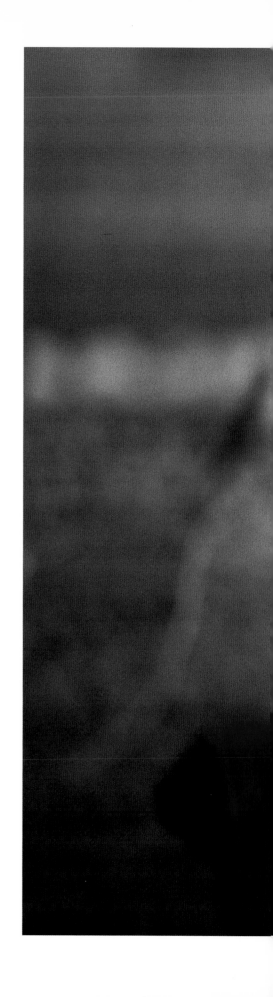

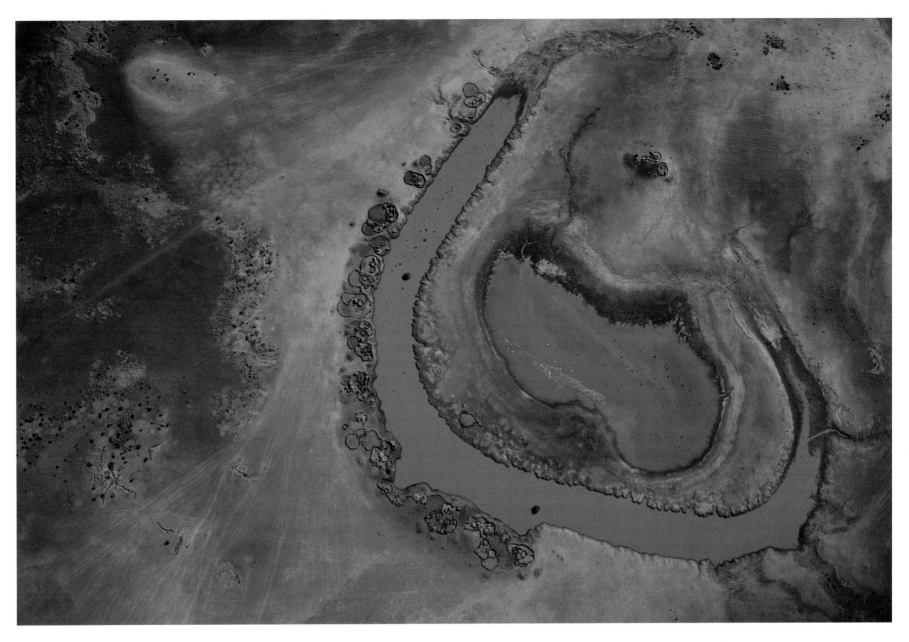

(previous pages)
A young Afar girl strolling about the desert in north-east Ethiopia, where the lava is exposed to strong hot winds, as she looks after her goats. Men herd camels and cattle, but women and children herd goats.

(opposite)
Much of the Danakil lowlands, inhabited by the Afar people, was once part of the Red Sea, and is the site of a vast salt plain. The people of Ethiopia have, since time immemorial, obtained *amolés*, or bars of salt traditionally used instead as money, from this area. The photograph shows part of the sea in the territory of Djibouti, in the foreground, and the Assal salt lake, 156 metres (512 feet) below sea level, in the background.

(above)
An oxbow lake, in the shape of a horse-shoe, formed by the Awash River changing its course.

A rugged tower of mud called Trabaartin rises in the sky on the shore of Lake Abbé, on the frontier between Ethiopia and Djibouti. The hillock was formed by an accumulation of mud hurled with boiling water from the ground, and is as hard as rock, as it contains a sizeable amount of calcium. In the foreground, note an Afar herd of goats.

Young Afar women do not cover their
breasts until after they are married.
Though Muslim, the covering of the
body, and the wearing of veils is unusual.

Afar men almost always carry guns when
they leave their camps to accompany
their herds.

139

Men praying after sunset. A large number of cattle, which were taken out for grazing, return at sunset in a cloud of dust as the wind dies down.

(opposite)
Young girls stay in camp in the early morning.

(above)
Men and women both often have a sharp look, possibly resulting from the insecurity of daily life in a naturally hostile environment.

A young Afar man, who had taken the
cattle for grazing, returns to camp in the
early evening. Afar men almost always
carry daggers for self-protection.

The nomads' everyday foods are goats'
milk and bread.

Women place dough on a metal plate in
a hole, and light a fire above it to bake
the bread. Since no leavening agent such
as yeast is used, the bread tends to be
hard.

(above)
Women carry drinking water in bags made of goats' skin. Water, in the vicinity of the Awash river, is often found by digging in the sand to a depth of about five metres (16 feet).

(opposite)
A girl carrying water on her back. Prior to puberty, girls have their clitoris cut out, and their vagina stitched up. Old women cut the thread away before the woman's wedding ceremony.

The tent's interior is just large enough for the family to sleep in it. The tent is dark inside to keep out the sun, and heat. The tent's hem is rolled up in late afternoon, as the sunlight becomes softer. The articles hanging from the roof are made of goats' skin.

Afar men carry guns as if they were walking sticks. Here in the Horn of Africa, disputes have never ceased, and the government has never attempted to control Afar guns.

An Afar woman.

Collecting salt at Lake Assal in Djibouti. This salt, in the form of small pieces or powder, is transported in sacks, whereas that in Dallol, the northern Danakil lowlands, is cut and transported in solid blocks.

Salt excavated in Dallol is transported by camel to Mekele, the administrative capital of Tegray region.

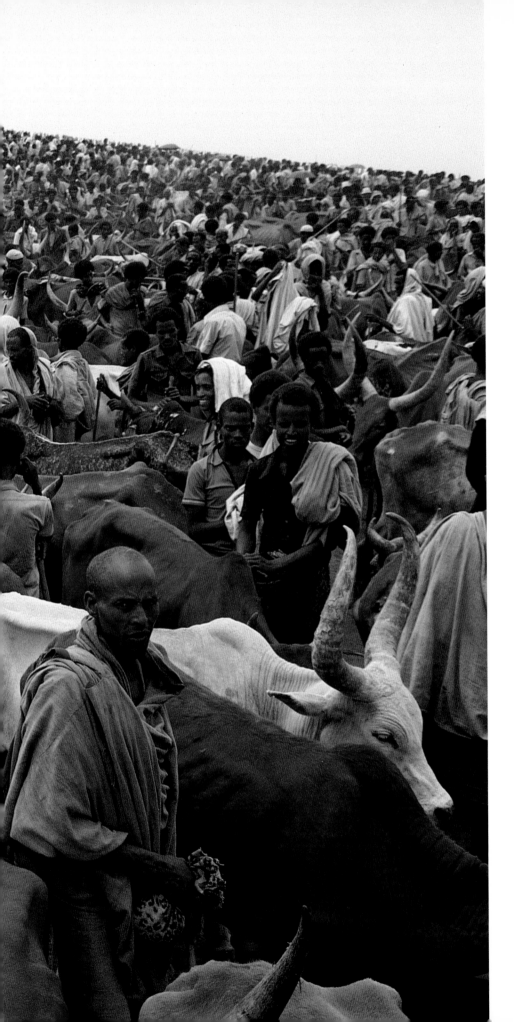

(*above*)
A gallows, still standing at Bati market. Public hangings were formerly a means of ensuring public order.

(*opposite*)
A herd of cattle on sale in Bati market, in the north-east of the country. The picture was taken in 1984, after three years of drought, when the livestock were underfed. Fearing that their cattle would die of starvation, owners sought to sell them at any price. A great famine was to follow.

155

OMO VALLEY

The Omo River of south-west Ethiopia runs in a southerly direction for almost 1,000 kilometres without reaching the sea, eventually losing itself in Lake Turkana on the Kenya frontier. The river begins on the cool plateau before proceeding through savanna country to the torrid deserts of Ethiopia's southern borderlands. Over the millennia, the river's waters have cut immense gorges, and innumerable wild game and colourful birds have come to inhabit its banks. The nearby Omo National Park, in particular, is the home of numerous lion, buffalo, and elephant, as well as oryx, giraffe, zebra, hartebeest, gerenuk, and gazelle.

The lower stretches of the Omo are inhabited by a remarkable variety of small but culturally interesting ethnic groups with different languages, ways of life, and customs. The most important of these peoples are the Bumé, Karo, Galeb, Bodi, Mursi, Surma, Arboré, and Hamar.

All these peoples have their own, often unique, artistic forms of expression and personal adornment. The Karo and Surma use clay and locally available vegetable dyes to paint their bodies and decorate each other's faces with fantastic patterns. The Mursi carve deep crescent incisions on their arms, to create patterns in scars. Mursi and Surma women insert large wooden and terra cotta 'lip plates' into their mouths, as well as disks into their ear lobes.

Hairstyle is another form of artistic expression of peoples of the Omo area. Hamar women wear their hair down in dense strips thickened with butter and mud and decorated, over their foreheads, with elongated strips of bright aluminum. Galeb and Karo men sculpt and shave their hair into complicated shapes, with ochre 'caps' of hair, adorned with ostrich feathers.

The Omo menfolk also have dramatic ceremonies, such as ritual stick-fighting, which add excitement to everyday life and win them admiration from their nubile sisters.

(previous pages)
Young men of the Galeb people, who came to the Omo River in the south-west of the country to water their cattle in the late afternoon. They are watching the river, on the look-out for its many crocodiles. Note sparse clothing, and the individual in the centre with a key—a sign of modernity—affixed to his necklace.

(above)
A Galeb man swimming in the Omo River, which reflects the sunset in the sky. The countryside in the Omo area is low-lying and therefore hot; the humidity high. Since temperatures during the day become unbearable, the Galebs often bathe and relax their dusty bodies in the refreshing river water.

A man's hair is hardened with clay. The attachment on the top of his forehead is intended to hold ostrich feathers or other ornaments. When the hair grows it is necessary, as shown in these pictures, to rearrange this hair attachment.

A man of the Banna people takes a nap. His hairstyle indicates that he has been victorious in war, or hunting. Use of the wooden pillow ensures that his hairstyle is not crumpled while sleeping.

A unique rite of passage ritual among the Hamar people is that of the Jumping of the Bull. As part of their passage to manhood, young men are supposed to run and jump four times over the backs of 20 bulls. He who fails will be laughed at by the women.

The Jumping of the Bull ceremony is accompanied by that of the Whipping of the Women. A woman will stand in front of a man who is holding a long twig, and will quietly allow him to beat her. After each stroke the twig is thrown away, and not used again. The more scars a woman has on her back, the more coming of age rituals her family has held, and the more prosperous it is therefore accounted.

A coffee ritual. The drink is brewed not from the beans of the coffee, but from its husks. After the blowing of horns, the women stamp their feet in rhythm, praising the bravery of the young men who are about to compete in the Jumping of the Bull ceremony.

Dance of the Hamar people. Such dances are usually held during the rainy season, when the pasture lands are blooming. As they dance the men gradually approach the women, until the hips of the two sexes touch. The men then make various gestures suggesting love-making, after which they draw away, only to repeat the previous manoeuvre time and time again, for many hours at a stretch.

Women, with brightly painted faces, sing rhythmically as they rub their arms together.

While the women dance barefoot, the
men jump up and down in sandals.
This makes a banging sound, which
reverberates through the night. Some
couples then disappear into the bush.

Hamar women, some with their children,
gather together for grain distribution by
a non-governmental organisation. Married
women wear a special type of collar, or
necklace, and handle, called *binyale*, like
that worn by the woman in the centre of
the picture. They continue to wear these
collars as long as the marriage lasts. Note
also cowry shells.

(above)
The Hamar people believe that it brings bad luck if a child's upper front teeth grow before his lower ones. Children in the old days were sometimes abandoned for this reason, and even today villagers may seek to give away such children to a neighbouring people.

(opposite)
Among women in the Omo area unmarried women can take part freely in sexual intercourse. In the event of pregnancy, the women are expected to practice abortion, or abandon the children. On the other hand, after marriage all children—even those of a man other than her husband—are accepted, without distinction, as a member of the family.

Though nearly naked, which is not surprising in this hot climate, many men are the proud owners of Kalashnikov rifles. Such weapons, because of the civil war in the neighbouring Sudan, are far from difficult to come by.

Clothes made of cattle skin, decorated
with numerous cowry shells, and metal
necklaces and armlets are common
among the women of the Omo area.
Some men wear cotton T-shirts, but
cloth has not yet spread among the
female half of the population.

Young Mursi men, some with necklaces and armlets, enjoy the board-game *Huroy*, known in Amharic as *Gabata*. Variations of this game are played all over Ethiopia, as well as in many other parts of Africa, and even India.

A young Galeb girl milking a goat. She is holding one of the animal's rear legs between her calf and thigh.

Karo girls waiting for the dance to commence.

A Hamar woman running to escape a
rain shower. The Hamar, who live by
grazing cattle in arid scrubland, normally
welcome the coming of the rains. During
the dry season, the grass becomes
parched, and the branches which the
cattle eat lose their leaves.

184

A cool sunset after a squall.

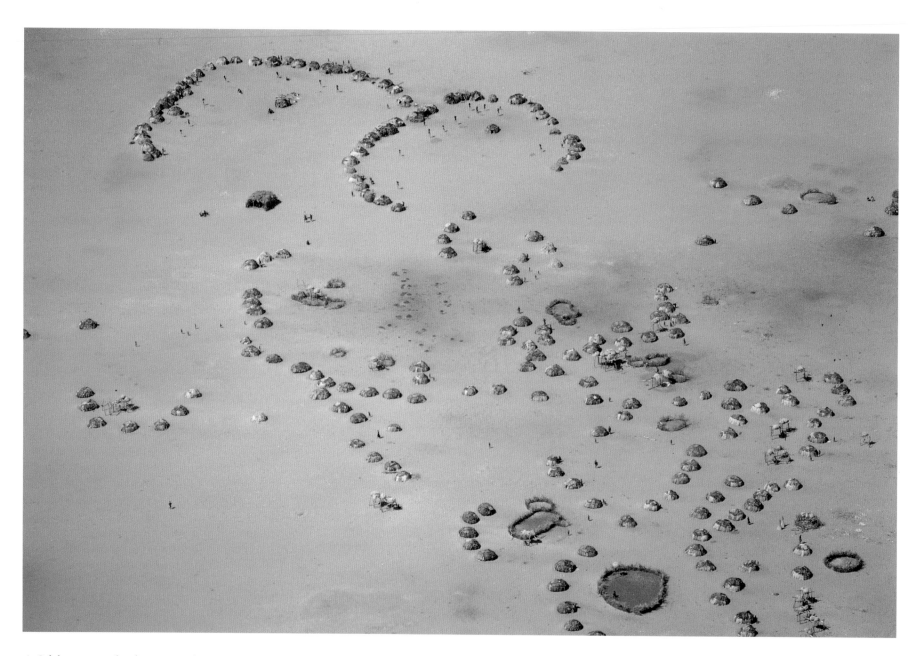

A Galeb camp in the desert near the Omo River. The photographer's Cessna pilot was reluctant to fly lower, as the local people were suspected of having acquired numerous firearms.

A Konso village covered with houses and other buildings. Their configuration resembles the contour lines on a map. There are about seven such Konso villages, this one with a population of about 3,000 inhabitants.

(top)
In Konso villages the houses with cone-shaped thatched roofs stand so close together that there is only a one-metre (three-foot) path between them. All houses, without exception, are surmounted by clay pots.

(bottom)
Konso youths spinning cotton. As soon as the photographer entered the village he was surrounded by so many children that he could not take any more pictures.

(opposite)
A young Konso woman cultivating the land, with a simple pick. Her people are expert at terracing, which is perhaps unrivalled anywhere in Africa.

(opposite)
Konso wooden carved figures, called *wagas*, enshrined at the entrance to a village. They commemorate the dead. It is sad that many are currently being dug up and taken to the Ethiopian capital, for sale to tourists.

(above)
Corpse of a Konso elder tied to a pole. He has a *kalicha*, or phallic symbol, attached to his forehead. Close friends and neighbours often spend the night with the dead like this, while others outside the house sing, praising the longevity of the deceased.

(left)
A young, beautifully dressed, Borana girl. The Boranas, who live in the far south of the country, beyond the Omo River, are a nomadic, Oromo-speaking people, who extend far into the northern province of Kenya.

(right)
Deep wells, sometimes as much as 50 metres (164 feet) deep, support the cattle in the arid Borana lands. Water is handed up in containers from person to person. These wells are sometimes called Singing Wells, as the men, to enliven their work, are constantly singing.

(left)
A watering place for the livestock, 20 metres (66 feet) down from ground level, reached by a special cattle path. Several men stand by its entrance to control the rush of thirsty cattle seeking water.

(right)
Water is passed by hand from person to person, in buckets or polythene containers. The Boranas draw water from these wells almost all day throughout the dry season. Most of the songs they sing while drawing water are to honour the cattle.

(opposite)
Since water in the deeper wells cannot easily be carried all the way up, intermediary pools are often made. On reaching the area the photographer heard the singing voices of the Boranas rising, like smoke, from the bottom of the well.

Chaw Bét, literally Salt House, a huge, 300 metre (984 feet) deep crater lake of salt water in Borana. As the water evaporates, during the three or four months at the peak of the dry season when evaporation is at its greatest, Borana men go out in the water with sticks, to collect salt from the bottom of the shallower parts of the lake. They work naked, for the salt would soon destroy their clothes.

197

Boranas, living in a village near Chaw Bét, have for many generations earned their living entirely from salt. A man carries salt-impregnated mud from part of the lake bottom. He scoops it up in his hands, without the use of a trowel or other tools, which would not survive in the saline water. Men walk up and down the steep crater and work hard, without stopping for lunch. The heat is intense, and there is no shade at all at the bottom of the crater.

199

The Modernization of an Ancient Realm

The modernization of Ethiopia began only in the second half of the 19th century, and did not make much headway until the first years of the 20th century.

The 20th century, when economic development began in neighbouring Egypt, was a difficult time. The Ethiopian heartlands were divided into several independent and mutually hostile provinces. Access to the sea was likewise far from easy, for the coast was dominated by hostile foreign powers.

The first significant attempts at innovation in Ethiopia were made by Emperor Téwodros, or Theodore, II. Formerly known as Kasa, his ambition was to restore Ethiopia's past greatness. An impetuous ruler, he tried to crush the provincial chiefs, and bring the entire country under his control. This led to strong opposition from the nobility. They were supported by the clergy, whom he had alienated by threats to confiscate Church lands, for the upkeep of his troops.

Deeply aware of the need to bolster his military strength, he tried to obtain assistance from the British government. He wrote to Queen Victoria in 1862, to propose co-operation. The British, however, were allied to the Turks and Egyptians, who had annexed Ethiopian territories claimed by Téwodros. The British, reluctant to become involved, left his letter unanswered. After waiting some years in vain he responded by imprisoning the British consul, and several other Europeans. The British government eventually replied to the letter, and agreed to recruit craftsmen for the Emperor. Before these could arrive, however, their relations seriously deteriorated. Britain despatched an armed expedition against Téwodros's mountain citadel, Maqdala. The Emperor, defeated in battle, released his European prisoners, but the British insisted on his unconditional surrender, whereupon he committed suicide. With his death in April 1868, his modernization plans came to an end.

Téwodros's successor, Emperor Yohannes IV (1872–1889), though somewhat conservative, was also aware of the need for modernization. More successful than Téwodros as a unifier, he incorporated the northern provinces under his rule. He was, however, confronted by a series of foreign invasions: by the Egyptians, in the 1870s, and by both the Italians and Sudanese Dervishes in the following decade. He achieved two remarkable victories over the Egyptians, and held his other enemies at bay. Constant fighting, however, rendered it impossible for him to embark on much innovation. He was killed fighting the Dervishes in March 1889, the last crowned head to die in battle.

Modernization was thus largely deferred until the time of Menilek II, who reigned as king of Shewa from 1865–89, and thereafter as Emperor until 1913. Menilek, a keen supporter of innovation, established Ethiopia's present capital, Addis Ababa, in 1887, and carried out a number of expeditions, which brought the southern provinces under his control. In the next few years, he reformed the taxation system, instituted the country's first national currency and postage stamps, sent a few students for study abroad, and granted a concession for the Djibouti railway. Further progress, however, was subsequently retarded by conflict with the Italians. This was resolved only by Ethiopia's resounding victory at the battle of Adwa in March 1896.

Most of Menilek's modernization was thus achieved only in the first decade of the 20th century, when the modern Ethiopian state was founded. This period witnessed the building of the country's first modern roads, the construction of the Djibouti railway, the introduction of a telephone-telegraph system, and the founding of a bank, and a printing press, as well as the establishment of the first modern schools and hospitals, the coming of the first motor car, and the appointment in 1907 of the first Cabinet. The Emperor's health then failed, after which a succession struggle militated against reform.

Significant progress was resumed only after the accession, in 1916, of Menilek's daughter, Empress Zawditu. Progress owed much to the interest in reform of the then Regent and Heir to the Throne, Tafari Makonnen, the future Emperor Haile Sellassie I. The ensuing period witnessed an expansion in the ministerial system, and road network, the founding of new schools and hospitals and the despatch of more students for study abroad. The country joined the League of Nations in 1923. In the following year the first of two anti-slavery decrees was issued, and the Regent embarked on a major European tour. The country's first aeroplane arrived in 1929.

After Haile Sellassie's coronation in 1930, the tempo of progress increased. Developments included the further expansion of roads, schools, hospitals and the ministerial system, reform of land tenure and taxation, nationalisation of the hitherto foreign-owned bank, a second anti-slavery edict and the establishment of the first radio station, as well as of a written Constitution, and the opening of a Parliament.

Progress was once again interrupted, a few years later, by the impending Italian Fascist invasion, and subsequent war. After their occupation, which brought Ethiopia and the Italian colonies of Eritrea and Somalia under a single administration, the invaders embarked on an ambitious road-building programme, extensive urban housing and some limited industrial development. Their rule, which was bitterly resisted by the Ethiopian Patriots, was, however, too short to achieve much in other fields. The Fascist bureaucracy was corrupt and inefficient. Trade stagnated, and attempts to settle Italians on the land proved a costly failure. Fascist policy, based on rigid racial discrimination, deliberately curtailed 'native' education, thus seriously hindering post-war progress.

Ethiopia was liberated in 1941, after which the Emperor and his government, with the war still waging in Europe, began the daunting task of reconstruction. A new state bank was established in 1942, and a national currency in 1945. The first air services, by Ethiopian Airlines, were inaugurated in the following year. The first post-war school opened in 1943, and the first institution of higher learning, the University College of Addis Ababa, in 1950. It became the nucleus, together with several other colleges, of Haile Sellassie I (later Addis Ababa) University, founded in 1961. Several new factories and plantations were also established.

Economic development continued under the Emperor for the next three decades, a period of peace and prosperity virtually unprecedented in the country's modern history. This phase of the country's life came to an end with the Ethiopian Revolution of 1974, the consequences of which await scholarly evaluation.